CLAUDIA JONES
CHANGE-MAKER

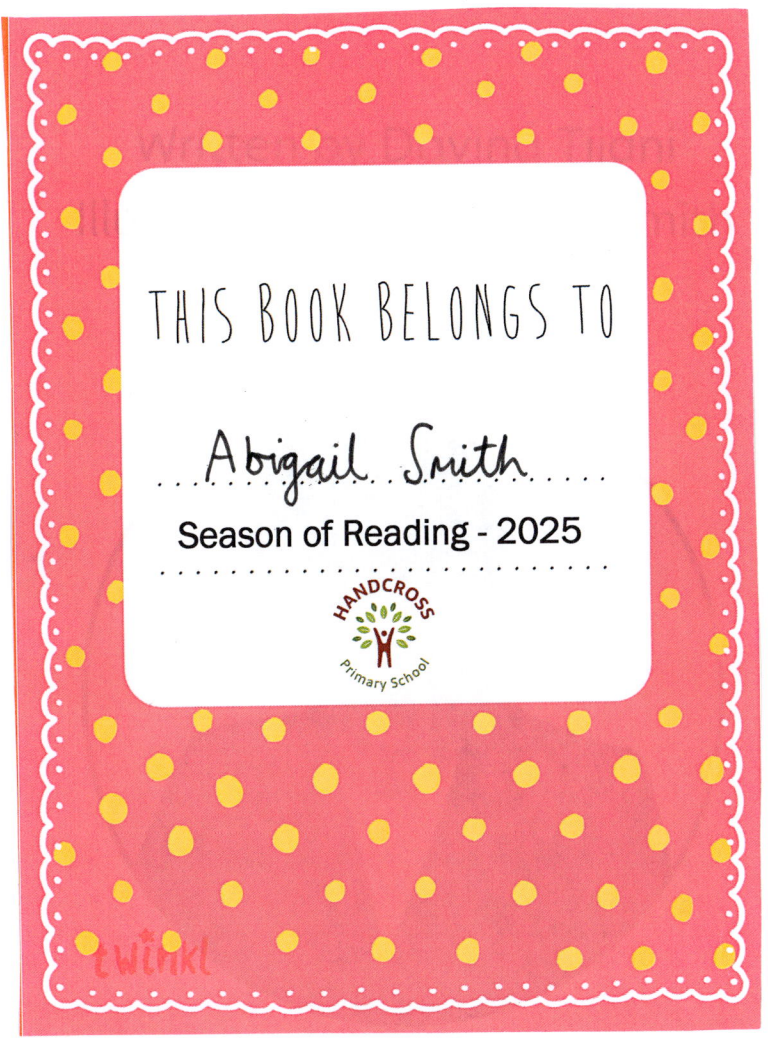

THIS BOOK BELONGS TO

Abigail Smith

Season of Reading - 2025

HANDCROSS Primary School

twinkl

OXFORD
UNIVERSITY PRESS

Words to look out for ...

allege *(verb)*
alleges, alleging, alleged
To allege that someone has done something is to accuse them of it, usually without proof.

authority *(noun)*
the power to give orders or to take action

bias *(noun)*
Bias is a strong feeling in favour of one person or side, or against another.

convenient *(adjective)*
suiting your needs; easy to use or deal with or reach

divert *(verb)*
diverts, diverting, diverted
To divert someone's attention is to make them think about something different.

guidance *(noun)*
information or advice on how to do something

likelihood *(noun)*
the chance of something happening; how likely something is to happen

mode *(noun)*
a particular way of behaving or of doing something

petition *(noun)*
a written request for something, usually signed by a large number of people

selective *(adjective)*
affecting or involving some people or things, but not others

Contents

A Black icon 4

Claudia's early life 6

Claudia in Harlem 10

The power of words 14

Putting words into action 16

Forced from the US 20

Life in 1950s London 21

Introducing the Windrush generation 23

Making Black voices heard 27

The West Indian Gazette 30

Claudia in the UK 35

Increasing tension 36

Mother of the Carnival 38

Making a difference 42

Later years 44

How Claudia's work lives on 45

Glossary 47

Index 48

A Black icon

History sometimes forgets its heroes; the people who fought bravely for the rights of others. One of those heroes was Claudia Jones, who came to live in the United Kingdom (UK) in 1955. Her actions during the years after World War Two (WW2) helped reshape modern society around the world.

Claudia Jones

Claudia Jones fought for civil rights. These are the rights that everyone living in a country has; for example, the right to vote, to be educated, and to be treated equally.

Claudia Jones is deservedly known as a change-maker; someone who takes action to solve a social problem and changes society for the better. She is not as well-known as other civil rights heroes, such as Rosa Parks or Doctor (Dr) Martin Luther King Junior (Jr). However, she also fought for equality and freedom.

TURN TO PAGE 18 TO LEARN ABOUT ROSA PARKS AND DR MARTIN LUTHER KING JR.

Claudia grew up in the United States (US). She saw how **racism** impacted Black people. She dedicated herself to standing up for the Black community, especially Black women.

Claudia could see that people experienced **discrimination** for more than one reason – such as their **ethnicity**, gender and **class**. This is known as intersectionality. People are made up of more than one identity and can suffer from more than one form of discrimination. This often leads to them experiencing further disadvantages in society.

Claudia showed a deep understanding of this through her work. Her actions led her to stand up:

- against racism
- against discrimination based on gender or class
- for independence.

Claudia became an activist – someone who takes action to bring about change to improve the lives of others. She wanted to create the change she knew the world needed.

Claudia's early life

Claudia was born in 1915 in Port of Spain, the capital city of Trinidad. Trinidad is part of the Republic of Trinidad and Tobago – an island nation in the Caribbean. When Claudia was born, Trinidad was a British colony; this meant it was under Britain's control.

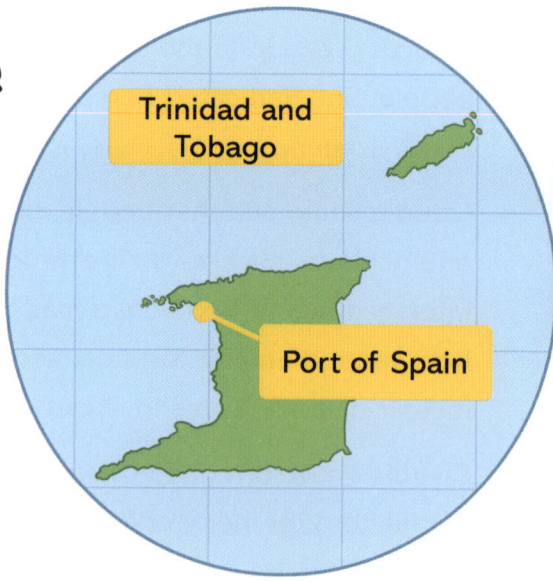

 What is a colony?
A colony is when one country takes control of another country, ruling it and using the colonized country's resources to make money.

Claudia grew up in a loving home with her parents and sisters. She spent her early childhood living in Belmont, which is famous for its Carnival celebrations.

Carnival is an important part of Trinidad's culture. It is a festival where people dress up in brightly coloured costumes and parade through the streets, playing music and dancing. Claudia experienced the joy of Carnival from a young age.

Trinidad has forests, mountains and plains.

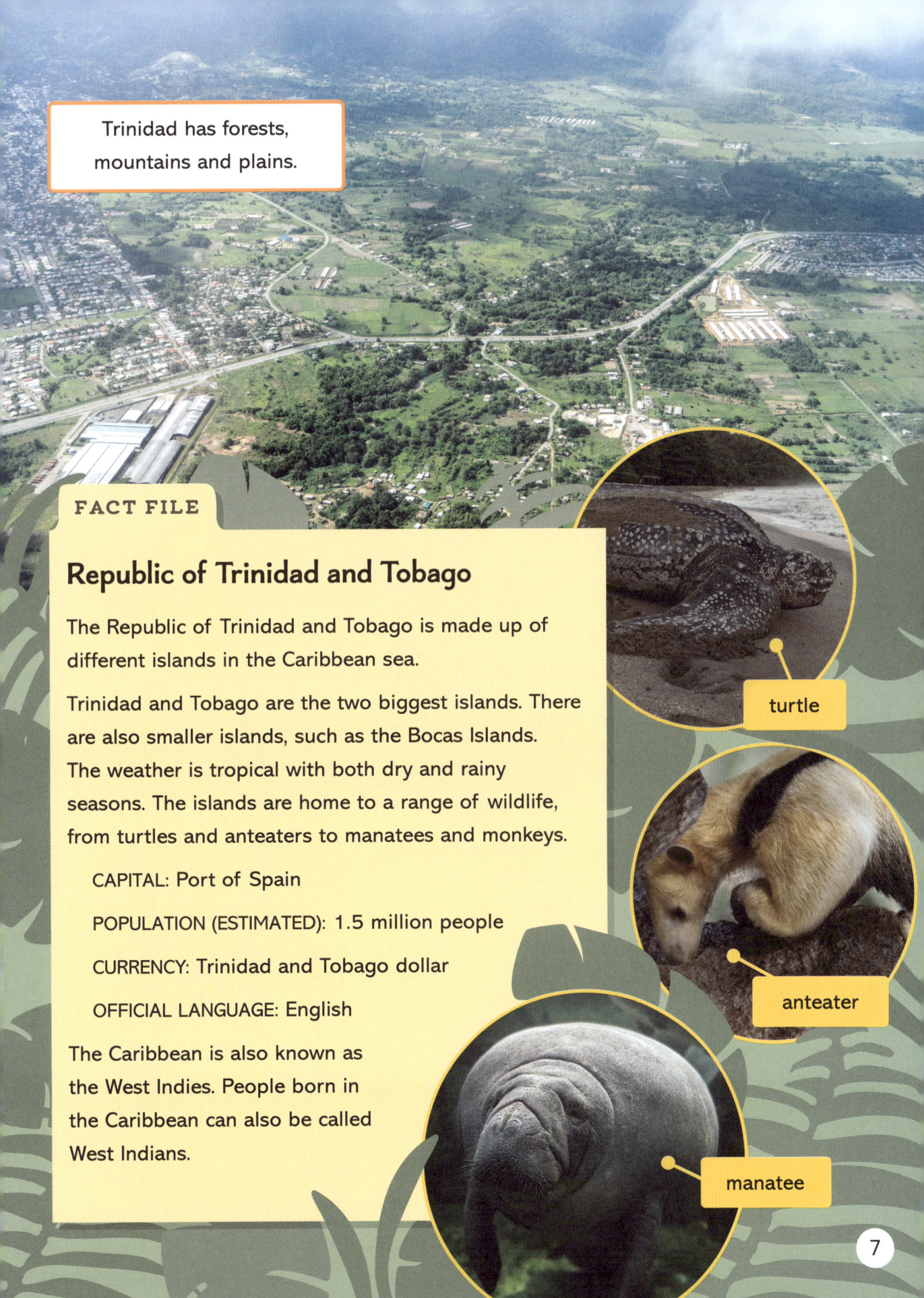

turtle

anteater

manatee

FACT FILE

Republic of Trinidad and Tobago

The Republic of Trinidad and Tobago is made up of different islands in the Caribbean sea.

Trinidad and Tobago are the two biggest islands. There are also smaller islands, such as the Bocas Islands. The weather is tropical with both dry and rainy seasons. The islands are home to a range of wildlife, from turtles and anteaters to manatees and monkeys.

- CAPITAL: Port of Spain
- POPULATION (ESTIMATED): 1.5 million people
- CURRENCY: Trinidad and Tobago dollar
- OFFICIAL LANGUAGE: English

The Caribbean is also known as the West Indies. People born in the Caribbean can also be called West Indians.

Trinidad was known for its cocoa which was used to make chocolate. In the 1920s, fewer countries wanted to buy cocoa. The whole of Trinidad suffered and people became poorer. Claudia's family decided they had to move elsewhere.

Claudia's parents moved first. They **emigrated** to the US. In 1924, Claudia, her sisters, and their aunt, travelled to Harlem, an area of New York City, to join them. Life in fast-paced Harlem was very different to the relaxed atmosphere of Port of Spain. Harlem had busy streets, large crowds, and non-stop traffic. It bustled with shops, newspapers, beauty salons, bars, and restaurants owned by Black people.

New York's Harlem pictured in the 1920s.

Claudia speaks

"Like thousands of West Indian **immigrants**, my parents hoped to find their fortunes in America ..."

Claudia's parents worked hard to support their family. Despite this, Claudia's family had little money. Claudia grew up in poverty.

While living in Harlem, Claudia experienced the harsh realities of being Black in the US. During this time, **segregation** was the law in southern parts of the US – this meant Black people couldn't use the same facilities as white people, such as schools, parks and shops. Though this was not the case in northern cities, such as New York, Black people living there still experienced discrimination. It was harder to get a job and many lived in poor conditions.

Claudia was made to feel unwelcome because she was Black. The fact she was a woman *and* **working class** also contributed to the discrimination she faced.

Harlem apartment buildings

All these experiences shaped Claudia as she grew up and inspired her to find ways to make changes in the future.

Claudia in Harlem

In 1927, when Claudia was just 12 years old, her mother became very unwell and died. Despite this difficult experience, Claudia worked hard at school. Claudia and her sisters attended a school in Harlem where most of the other students were white.

The white students bullied Claudia and her sisters because they were Black. This was a hurtful experience for them. However, Claudia overcame this and was eventually elected mayor of the school by the other students.

Claudia won many school awards. She spent her time in social clubs and playing tennis. She also attended a drama group.

During her time at school, Claudia became interested in politics. This paved the way for Claudia to take her first steps into **activism**.

During the 1920s, the Black population of Harlem grew fast. The area went through a creative period known as the Harlem Renaissance. This 'rebirth' attracted Black people from other parts of the US and around the world. It occurred through several modes of expression including writing, music, art, fashion, theatre, and dance. Harlem was transforming and Claudia was at the heart of it.

FACT FILE

Harlem Renaissance creatives

AUGUSTA SAVAGE: Augusta was a sculptor who started creating art when she was young, using red clay to make animals. She went on to create many famous sculptures and have exhibits all around the world.

Augusta Savage

Duke Ellington

DUKE ELLINGTON: Duke was a jazz pianist and composer who created a distinctive sound. He played with his band for almost 50 years.

ZORA NEALE HURSTON: Zora was a writer and wrote many famous books. Her most recent work was published 62 years after her death, showing the ongoing impact she has had on American literature.

Zora Neale Hurston

A mode is a particular way of behaving or of doing something.

Claudia gets sick

When Claudia was 17 years old, she caught tuberculosis which impacted her for the rest of her life. To help her recover, Claudia was sent to a special hospital. Claudia stayed there for a year. This was a convenient time for her to think about what she would do with her life.

Claudia speaks

"There, too, I had the opportunity to read avidly, to think deeply, about the social ideas **instilled** in me by my mother and father."

FACT FILE

What is tuberculosis?

Tuberculosis is a disease that mostly affects the lungs. It is caused by **bacteria** that thrives in dark, damp, and crowded places. It was a problem for people living in poor conditions in 20th century New York. Tuberculosis spreads through the air from infected people's coughs, spit and sneezes.

SYMPTOMS: cough, fever, chest pain, breathlessness

TREATMENT: antibiotics (a type of medicine that kills bacteria)

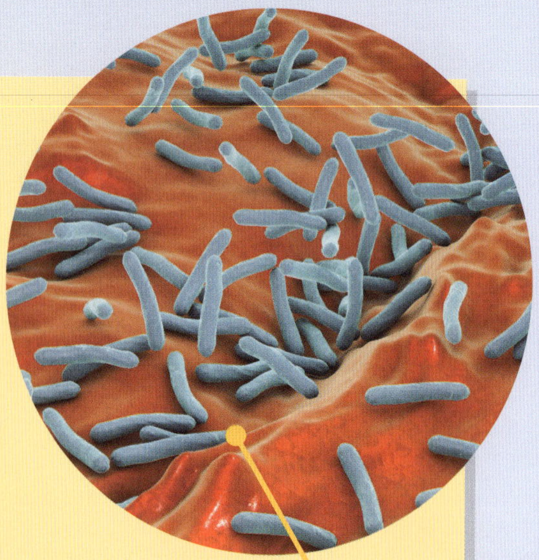

tuberculosis bacteria

Something is convenient when it suits your needs, or when it is easy to use or deal with or reach.

After Claudia recovered, she finished high school. However, she couldn't attend her **graduation** ceremony because her family couldn't afford to buy an outfit for her to wear to it.

During the 1930s, Black people – especially women – couldn't afford to go to university, received low pay, had poorer health and didn't live as long. Black working class women suffered from intersectionality. This made it particularly difficult for them to find opportunities to progress forward.

Due to being Black, a woman, working class *and* an immigrant, Claudia had even fewer opportunities. She was not able to go to university. After finishing school, Claudia worked in a laundry, a factory, a hat shop and as a saleswoman.

Claudia worked in a millinery shop selling hats.

The power of words

Claudia knew the importance of having a voice and how words could be used to make people feel seen and heard. She understood the power of spoken words but also valued another mode of communication – the written word. Claudia was inspired by her father. He had several jobs to support their family, but in his spare time, he was the editor of a newspaper called the *West Indian American*. (Turn to page 29 to find out more about what an editor does.) Claudia's father would have been an early role model for her own career as a journalist.

A newspaper stand in Harlem, 1939.

Around the age of twenty, Claudia started writing articles called *Claudia Comments* for a local Harlem magazine. This was her first job as a journalist. Claudia's articles were aimed at the Black community to keep them informed of what was happening, not only in the US but across the entire world.

A mode is a particular way of behaving or of doing something.

While working as a journalist, Claudia became interested in **public speaking**. She was inspired by the public speakers on the streets of Harlem.

Encouraged by what other civil rights activists were doing around her, Claudia became involved in campaigns to create social change. She fought against the serious **injustices** that were faced by immigrant people, Black people, and women. During the 20th century, feminism (the rights of women) was a huge discussion point in society. Women were campaigning for their voices to be heard and for an end to the bias they faced in education, the medical system, the legal system, and even at home.

Claudia travelled around the US organizing **rallies**. Her passion and ability to inspire others through her public speaking meant she succeeded in uniting people who shared similar **values**.

📢 What are campaigns?
A campaign is a plan of activities to bring about, or to stop, change in society.

Bias is a strong feeling in favour of one person or side, or against another.

Putting words into action

Claudia also believed in protection and rights for working class people. Using her passion for words, Claudia developed her writing and public speaking skills and organized community events.

In 1936, Claudia joined the Young Communist party. She felt that communism connected with her values.

What is communism?

Communism is a political system where the government or community owns and controls businesses, property, and land, rather than individuals or companies. It is based on a theory that each person works and is paid according to their abilities and needs.

Claudia later joined the Communist Party in the US and became an important member. As her journalism career grew, Claudia also contributed to and then became the editor of various political newspapers.

Other civil rights activists

Across the US, civil rights activists were working hard to achieve desegregation (the end of segregation). They used several methods.

Legal challenges: People challenge the law to create change.

EXAMPLE: In the 1950s, a legal challenge led to the desegregation of US schools in a case called *Brown vs Board of Education*. The separation of schools for Black and white children went against the law, which said that all people in similar situations should be treated in a similar way.

Lawyers celebrating their successful petition for the desegregation of schools.

Sit-ins: People occupy a public space as a way of protesting.

EXAMPLE: In the 1960s in Greensboro, US, Black university students asked to be served at a lunch counter in a shop. They were refused, so they stayed until the shop closed. They returned the next day with more students. This protest gained attention and support, including from white Americans, eventually leading to the desegregation of lunch counters.

The students during their sit-in.

A petition is a written request for something, usually signed by a large number of people.

Marches: Large groups of people march in protest.

EXAMPLE: During the *March on Washington for Jobs and Freedom* in 1963, 250 000 people marched for civil rights. Here, famous activist, Dr Martin Luther King Jr, gave his well-known 'I Have a Dream' speech.

Dr Martin Luther King Jr speaking at the *March on Washington for Jobs and Freedom* in 1963.

Boycotts: People no longer use a service or buy a product.

EXAMPLE: In the 1950s, the *Montgomery Bus Boycott* started when Rosa Parks and other Black women were arrested for refusing to give up their seats to white passengers on the bus. Then the entire Black population of Montgomery refused to use the buses until the bus system was desegregated.

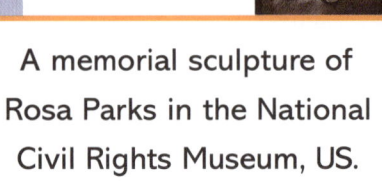

Rosa Parks started the *Montgomery Bus Boycott* on this bus in 1955.

A memorial sculpture of Rosa Parks in the National Civil Rights Museum, US.

Claudia gets arrested

Claudia fought for civil rights using the power of her words.

Claudia's activism drew the attention of the US government. They did not believe in communism. They criticized and arrested people who they alleged supported communism.

In 1948, aged 36, Claudia was sent to prison because of her activism. Sadly, while in prison, Claudia had a heart attack. She survived, but lived with a heart condition for the rest of her life.

In 1955, a petition was raised to stop her prison sentence. It was denied and Claudia was sent to prison again. After being released, the US government **deported** her. Claudia was not able to return to Trinidad, as the government there were worried that she might create problems. She had to leave the US to start a new life in a new country.

Claudia and other Communist Party members leaving court in 1951.

A petition is a written request for something, usually signed by a large number of people.
To allege that someone has done something is to accuse them of it, usually without proof.

Forced from the US

On 7th December 1955, Claudia boarded a boat and left New York for the UK. She had to leave behind her father and sisters. Despite being forced from the country she had lived in since she was a child, Claudia had inspired the people she left behind to create a better future for everyone.

In late December 1955, Claudia arrived in London.

Claudia struggled with her new home at first, falling very ill soon after arriving in London. She spent two months recovering in hospital.

Tragedy struck again when her father died. Due to her deportation, Claudia could not attend his funeral. Living in the UK, Claudia had to deal with all of this on her own without the guidance and support of her family and friends.

The River Thames in London, pictured in the 1950s.

Guidance is information or advice on how to do something.

Life in 1950s London

As Claudia settled in London, she continued with her fight for equality. She made contact with the Communist Party of Great Britain. However, the work she was given to do didn't match her vast experience and skills. Her relationship with the party in the UK was very different to her relationship with the Communist Party in the US. Claudia felt she didn't have as much involvement or authority.

She also felt some members of the party in the UK didn't understand the impact of racism on Black communities. They also didn't recognize their own racism towards Claudia. Seeing the huge problems faced by Black people in the UK, Claudia diverted her energy towards making sure the West Indian and other Black communities felt supported in the fight against racism. Claudia wanted to unite the Black community in the battle against racism, discrimination, and **prejudice**.

If you have authority, you have the power to give orders or to take action.
To divert someone's attention is to make them think about something different.

A nation in recovery

In 1945, after WW2, Europe was devastated. Buildings had been destroyed, many people had died, and food rationing continued.

Before the war, Britain had colonies around the world. Now some colonies had gained independence: they were no longer ruled by Britain, but were part of the Commonwealth.

FACT FILE

The Commonwealth

The Commonwealth is a group of 56 countries, including former British colonies and the UK.

WHY WAS IT FORMED? It began in 1926, as the British Empire began to break apart, to help keep connections between former colonies as they gained independence.

WHO IS PART OF THE COMMONWEALTH? Countries from Asia, Africa, Europe, Oceania, as well as the Caribbean.

In 1948, to help rebuild the country after the war, the UK government introduced the British Nationality Act. The law gave anyone who lived in a British colony the right to live and work in the UK.

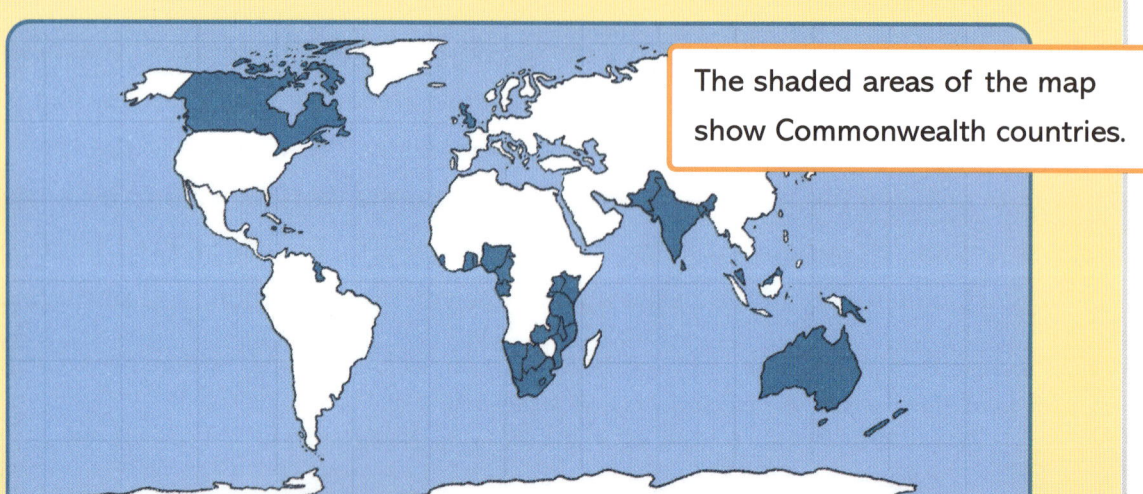

The shaded areas of the map show Commonwealth countries.

Introducing the Windrush generation

WHO ARE THE WINDRUSH GENERATION? They are the people who arrived in the UK from the Caribbean, between the end of WW2 and 1971. Many of them served in the British Armed Forces during WW2. They came from countries such as Jamaica, the Bahamas, Bermuda, British Guiana (now Guyana), and Trinidad and Tobago.

HOW DID THEY TRAVEL TO THE UK? The first group sailed from the Caribbean to the UK onboard a ship called Empire Windrush. This is why they are known as the Windrush generation.

WHEN DID THE EMPIRE WINDRUSH ARRIVE? On 21st June 1948, Empire Windrush arrived at Tilbury Docks in Essex, carrying 1027 men, women and children.

WHY DID THEY COME TO THE UK? For lots of different reasons, including a better standard of living. After WW2, the UK needed to be rebuilt. As there was a huge shortage of labour, the UK needed people to come and help with the rebuilding.

This map shows the route Empire Windrush took in 1948.

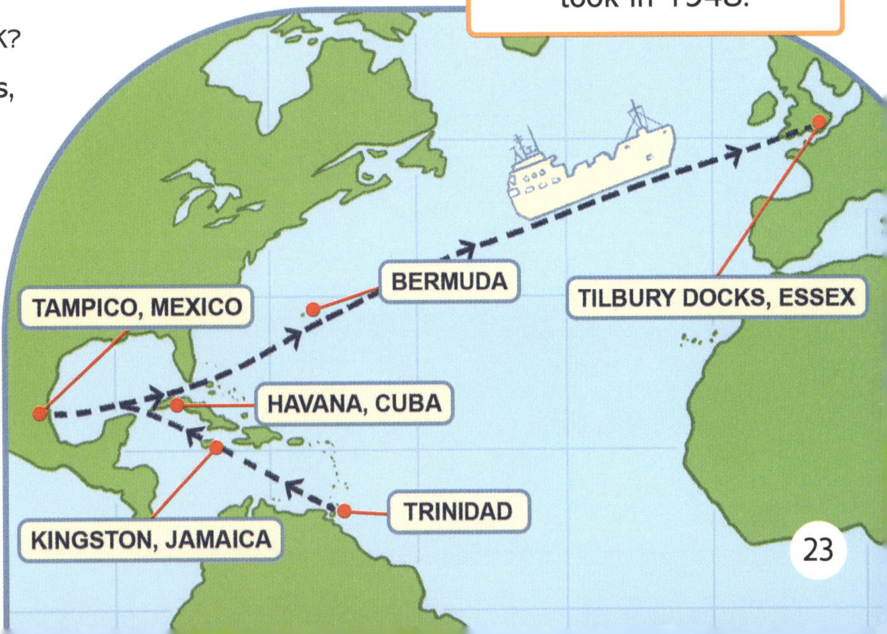

Life in the UK

Many of the Caribbean immigrants received an unfriendly welcome. Most of the new arrivals were treated poorly and couldn't find suitable places to live or work despite having the right skills and experience. **Organizations** who should have provided support and guidance didn't. Some opportunities did present themselves such as jobs working for the UK's health service, the railways, and buses.

The new arrivals had thought of the UK as the 'mother country', however the racism they experienced changed the way many felt. Even so, lots of them stayed, determined to make happy lives for themselves and their families.

FACT FILE

Windrush Day

Since 2018, Windrush Day has been held on 22nd June every year, to remember the arrival of Caribbean passengers on board Empire Windrush. It is an opportunity to celebrate their lives, and their contribution to the UK.

The National Windrush Monument is in Waterloo Station, London.

Guidance is information or advice on how to do something.

Claudia immediately connected with the new arrivals from the Caribbean. She wanted to improve the way the immigrant Black community in the UK was treated. Claudia hoped to continue the work she had done in the US, having seen what activism could accomplish.

Organizations were formed to help gain equal rights for Black communities living in the UK. Claudia became a member of several of them. She joined in with their work to deal with increasing **tensions** and to challenge the problems which affected Black people from across the UK.

Claudia attended and spoke at events and talks, such as a meeting on African Women's Day in 1961.

Being a Black person in the UK in the 1950s was very different to being a white person. Racial bias in the UK was strong and it was common for racist people to target Black people just because they were Black. This caused tension between the different communities around the country. Black people were refused service in restaurants, shops, and other businesses. This was known as a 'colour bar'.

Black women faced further discrimination due to their gender. In the past, women had not been expected to work outside of the home. However, during WW2 women were needed to take on jobs previously carried out by men. Despite the increase in the number of women working during the 1950s, many jobs continued to be seen as 'men's jobs'. It was still uncommon for women to go to university. These limitations were even more of an issue for Black women. Class also had an influence on the opportunities women had.

Women worked in factories, offices, and in health care.

Bias is a strong feeling in favour of one person or side, or against another.

Making Black voices heard

As Claudia understood, all these factors – ethnicity, gender and class – shape a person's identity and life experiences. When a person's identity includes more than one of these factors, they are more likely to face discrimination.

Claudia realized the most important part of her mission to create change for Black communities was to ensure their voices were always heard.

To achieve this, she wanted to create a safe space and a powerful platform to lift up their voices. She believed by doing so she could ensure different types of discrimination, from racism to gender and class inequality, would be addressed properly. Once again, Claudia turned back to the power of words to achieve this. She decided a newspaper would be a powerful and convenient solution to reaching as many people as possible.

Something is convenient when it suits your needs, or when it is easy to use or deal with or reach.

Claudia decided the Black community needed its own newspaper. She wanted to create a paper that would be aimed at the UK's growing West Indian population and focused on the issues which most impacted them. The newspaper's full name was the *West Indian Gazette and Afro-Asian Caribbean News* but was better known as the *West Indian Gazette* or *WIG*. This was the one of the first major Black newspapers in the UK.

Claudia knew the power of giving Black people a platform to speak from and be heard. She hoped the newspaper would encourage conversations between Black people about the problems they were facing around the world.

How to set up a newspaper

1. Decide who your readers will be and what topics you want to cover, for example films, politics, sports, or general news.

2. Create a team! You will need:

   - an editor-in-chief – the boss of the newspaper who oversees everything
   - a news editor – the person who oversees the content for the newspaper
   - a photographer – to take photographs for the events in the newspaper
   - a reporter – the person who writes the stories
   - a sub-editor – the person who checks the spelling and grammar of the news stories, and thinks about the page layout and writes the headlines.

3. Decide how often you will publish your newspaper. Will it be daily, weekly, biweekly (every two weeks), or monthly?

4. How long will your newspaper be?

5. Choose a snappy name for your newspaper.

6. Start writing! Think of headlines, types of articles and look for photos.

The West Indian Gazette

Claudia developed the newspaper with Amy Ashwood Garvey, a well-known activist. In 1958, they set up the newspaper headquarters above a record shop in Brixton, South London. Claudia was the editor-in-chief of the newspaper. The *WIG* was published monthly, with its first issue coming out in March 1958. Claudia struggled to get funding for the newspaper, so it relied on people who were willing to write articles for free.

The newspaper covered the news, but also featured Caribbean arts and culture. It included book reviews, poems and recommendations of West Indian restaurants, shops, and clubs to visit in London.

Claudia's lifelong mission to inspire the Black community to create change focused on several different areas.

Claudia used the *WIG* to address these topics, as they impacted the quality of life for the entire community. Claudia understood the need to challenge and change the negative atmosphere that existed for Black people in the UK.

Claudia used the newspaper's offices to conduct interviews and meetings with politicians, academics, and activists, including leaders from Jamaica and Trinidad and Tobago. By featuring the voices of Black leaders around the world, readers could see the problems they were facing in the UK were similar to problems faced all around the world.

Claudia put together a team to help create the newspaper.

Amy Ashwood Garvey

BORN IN: Jamaica

ROLE: Amy helped set up the paper with Claudia.

NEWSFLASH: She dedicated her life to supporting Black people around the world. She established the Afro-Women's Centre in London which provided support and education for women of African heritage.

Jan Carew

BORN IN: Guyana

ROLE: As Contributing Editor, Jan wrote articles for the newspaper.

NEWSFLASH: He was also an author, playwright, and poet.

Donald Hinds

BORN IN: Jamaica

ROLE: As City Reporter, Donald investigated stories and conducted interviews.

NEWSFLASH: Donald trained as a teacher in Jamaica but couldn't get a teaching job when he arrived in London. Instead, he became one of London's first Black bus conductors.

Abhimanyu Manchanda

BORN IN: India

ROLE: As General Manager, he had the authority to oversee the running of the paper.

NEWSFLASH: Abhimanyu was also a teacher and an activist, dedicated to fighting racism. He met Claudia when he joined the Communist Party of Great Britain.

James Fairweather

BORN IN: Jamaica

ROLE: As the Advertising Manager, James managed the advertising and marketing of the *WIG*.

NEWSFLASH: He asked local furniture shops to support the paper by paying the *WIG* to feature adverts for their shops in the paper. This helped to raise money to keep the paper going.

Sam King

BORN IN: Jamaica

ROLE: As Circulation Manager, Sam ensured people could buy the newspaper.

NEWSFLASH: He served in the Royal Air Force during WW2. After the war ended, he returned to Jamaica, before deciding to take the opportunity to return to the UK on board Empire Windrush. He later became Mayor of Southwark in London.

If you have authority, you have the power to give orders or to take action.

The impact of the newspaper

The newspaper's main mission was to place Black people at the centre of the news. Most of its readers were from the West Indian population, but the *West Indian Gazette* wanted to unite all Black immigrants regardless of their backgrounds.

The newspaper refused to be selective in what it reported. It informed readers of major events happening around the world. Readers responded positively to this global view of the world.

This included the civil rights movement in the US and the independence of British colonies in the Caribbean and in Africa.

Claudia tried to get the newspaper to change from a monthly to a weekly publication, as there was so much news to cover. However, due to a lack of funding, she was not able to make this happen.

A selective process affects or involves some people or things, but not others.

Claudia in the UK

Claudia built a positive reputation as an **advocate** for the right to fight against all forms of discrimination. Claudia organized marches, and gave public speeches to spread her message of freedom for everyone, everywhere.

FACT FILE

How did Claudia tackle issues?

ISSUE	WHAT DID CLAUDIA DO?
HOUSING Many West Indians lived in cramped, poor-quality houses and were charged high rents by their landlords.	✔ Claudia helped set up organizations to address housing inequality and other issues. ✔ Claudia campaigned with local politicians to obtain better housing options for the West Indian population.
DECOLONIZATION AND INDEPENDENCE Decolonization is when a country gains independence from another country. Many British colonies wanted independence to achieve political and **economic** freedom.	✔ Claudia met with Caribbean leaders in support of their work for independence.

A Jamaican father and his family in Brixton, an area of South London, in 1952.

Increasing tension

While Claudia was focused on the newspaper and raising awareness of the issues faced by Black people, tension was increasing. Riots erupted across Notting Hill – an area of London – in August 1958, with groups of white people targeting Black people. There were cases of houses being destroyed and the trouble spread to surrounding areas of London. The fighting and unrest carried on into September until the police regained control. Hundreds of people were arrested, and many were badly injured. There were similar riots in other cities across the UK, such as Nottingham, Bristol and Liverpool.

Notting Hill during the riots of 1958.

Finding a way forward

People were horrified by the riots. Questions were raised about racism and multiculturalism in the UK, and the impact of immigration on the country.

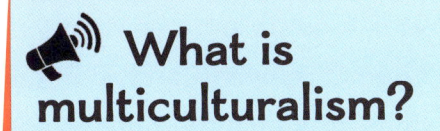

📣 What is multiculturalism?

Multiculturalism describes a society that is made up of people from different cultures.

The riots made community leaders think about what they could do to heal the damage. Claudia had a strong reputation for community organizing. She suggested they host a carnival to celebrate the beauty and excitement of Caribbean culture and the wider Black community. She hoped this would help **divert** attention in a more positive direction.

Claudia speaks

"A people's art is the **genesis** of their freedom."

To **divert** someone's attention is to make them think about something different.

Mother of the Carnival

In January 1959, Claudia and the *West Indian Gazette* team organized a huge Caribbean Carnival in London. It was held in the winter to match the timings of carnivals in the Caribbean, so it was held indoors instead of being a traditional street festival.

The Caribbean Carnival took place in St Pancras Town Hall, London on 30th January 1959.

Claudia wanted the Caribbean Carnival to present West Indian culture and talent to the public. There were fashion shows, steel bands, calypso music, dancing, and West Indian food.

The festival was shown live on television.

Calypso is West Indian folk music. It began in Trinidad in the 1800s.

Changing the narrative

Claudia hoped that the Caribbean Carnival would encourage tolerance, whereby people accept differences in beliefs, opinions and behaviour.

At first, such a large celebration was not well received by London newspapers. However, this didn't stop its success and more Caribbean Carnivals were held over the next five years around London. With each festival, popularity grew alongside increased understanding of West Indian culture, such as food, music, dance, and costumes.

Claudia speaks

"Our Carnival symbolises the unity of our people resident here and of all our many friends who love the West Indies."

These celebrations were a powerful way of getting others to learn about West Indian people, their history, and their culture. It helped to share a message of positivity and inclusion.

Claudia Jones became known as the Mother of the Carnival.

What happened next

The *WIG* Caribbean Carnivals paved the way for the Notting Hill Carnival – a festival first held in August 1966 in London.

Today, the Notting Hill Carnival is Europe's largest street festival. Local businesses and hotels benefit from the large number of visitors to the Notting Hill area. There is also an increase in jobs and volunteering roles for the local people. Every year, it attracts a global audience who come to see the colourful celebrations. Visitors attending the three-day festival spend money when buying food, drinks, clothes, and other items.

Since its early beginnings, the Notting Hill Carnival has continued to promote diversity, uplifting local communities through the power of celebrating culture and unity. Claudia's original Caribbean Carnival helped to plant the seeds from which the Notting Hill Carnival grew.

The history of the Notting Hill Carnival

1959
Claudia Jones and the *WIG* team help organize an indoor event known as the 'Caribbean Carnival'.

1960–1964
Annual 'Caribbean Carnivals' are held in halls across London.

1966
A Caribbean festival is held outside on the streets of Notting Hill for the first time.

1973–1975
The head of the Notting Hill Carnival encourages performers to wear traditional costumes, increases the number of steel pan bands and has larger sound systems.

1990s
Notting Hill Carnival begins to have international music acts appearing on its stages, including Black US stars.

Present day
The Notting Hill Carnival continues to take place every year on the last weekend of August. It is one of the largest street festivals in the world.

Making a difference

Claudia wanted to make a difference. She addressed problems faced by the most **oppressed** people and showcased them for the rest of the world to see.

She followed what was happening around the world, organizing rallies and other public demonstrations to protest against injustice. Despite being unable to return to the US, Claudia remained connected to her second home, especially in the fight for civil rights.

In August 1963, in support of the *March on Washington for Jobs and Freedom* led by Dr Martin Luther King Jr, Claudia led supporters on a civil rights march through London. When Dr Martin Luther King Jr won the 1964 Nobel Peace Prize, he came to Europe to collect his prize and met Claudia in London.

📢 What is the Nobel Peace Prize?

The Nobel Peace Prize is an award given out every year to someone who has worked for world peace.

Dr Martin Luther King Jr received the Nobel Peace Prize for his 'non-violent struggle for civil rights'.

Claudia always focused on the rights of Black people, immigrants, women and the working class in her activism. Her powerful campaigns were designed to bring about positive change to ensure all these groups had access to a better quality of life. Claudia did this by working with various organizations and politicians to generate support for campaigns against unfair laws which discriminated against these people.

> Claudia's lifelong work of activism was honoured with a special stamp from the Royal Mail – the national postal service in the UK.

Claudia is remembered for her strong leadership and activism which inspired people all around the world. Through her work, she showed how to stand up and fight discrimination in all its forms, ensuring no one was left behind.

There is a strong likelihood her achievements will encourage the next generation of change-makers to continue to fight for equality and freedom.

Likelihood is the chance of something happening or how likely something is to happen.

Later years

During the 1960s, Claudia travelled around the world to give speeches and talks (sometimes called lectures). She met powerful leaders and continued to champion the rights of women, attending the World Congress of Women in 1963.

However, Claudia's health in the final years of her life was poor. Sadly, she died in December 1964 at the age of 49. It is likely her early death was caused by her previous struggles with tuberculosis, along with the heart disease she developed after the heart attacks she suffered.

After her funeral, Claudia was laid to rest in Highgate Cemetery in North London.

This headstone marks Claudia's grave in North London.

How Claudia's work lives on

After Claudia died, the *West Indian Gazette* only survived for a few more months. However, the newspaper remained one of Claudia's most significant achievements.

Claudia's work lives on in many ways.

1. THE CLAUDIA JONES ORGANISATION: Founded in 1982, this organization is dedicated to supporting African Caribbean women and families in areas of London.

2. THE CLAUDIA JONES MEMORIAL LECTURE: This lecture is held every year by The National Union of Journalists' Black Members' Council to honour Claudia. The lecture always relates to the topics of Claudia's mission, such as racism, activism, and the importance of fighting injustice.

3. THE IMPORTANCE OF INTERSECTIONALITY: Claudia's work strengthened understanding of this important concept – how the mixture of different identities, including ethnicity, gender and class, affects the level of discrimination an individual can face.

Claudia Jones was a change-maker. She strove to make the world a more equal place for everyone – especially those who experienced discrimination. She fought constantly against racism, and for equal rights for working class people and for women. She stood for the values of freedom, unity, and multiculturalism. Throughout her life, Claudia showed immense spirit, determination and a strength of mind to overcome all the obstacles which stood in her way.

Claudia speaks

"Peace cannot be achieved if any woman, especially the oppressed and impoverished, is left out of the conversation."

In 2023, English Heritage honoured Claudia with a blue plaque. This award celebrates people who have contributed to the history of London. Claudia's blue plaque is in Vauxhall, London on the house Claudia used to live in.

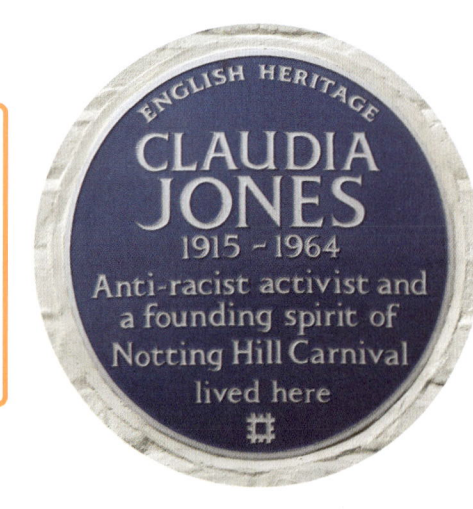

Glossary

activism: taking action to make or prevent a change, often to improve the way people live or are treated

advocate: a person who speaks in favour of someone or something

bacteria: tiny organisms that can cause diseases

class: a system of different ranks in society, also known as social class

deported: send someone out of a country

discrimination: treating people differently or unfairly because of their ethnicity, age, gender, disability, or religion

economic: to do with money

emigrated: when someone has left their own country to live in another country

ethnicity: a term that refers to groups of people with a shared identity such as culture, religion and language.

genesis: the beginning of something

graduation: when someone receives their university qualification

immigrants: people who have come into a country to live there

injustices: unfair actions or treatment

instilled: slowly but surely encouraged someone to think a certain way

oppressed: people who are ruled or treated in a cruel or unjust way

organizations: groups of people who work together to do something

prejudice: when someone decides that they do not like someone or something without a good reason or without thinking about it

public speaking: when someone addresses more than one person, expressing their opinions and ideas

racism: when people are treated unfairly because of their shared ancestry and physical features, such as black or brown skin; racism can take many different forms, for example bullying or being excluded from places, services, or activities

rallies: large meetings to show support for something

segregation: the separation of people of different ethnicities or religions

tensions: feelings created in situations when people are uneasy, nervous or do not trust one another

values: beliefs and ideas about what is right and wrong, or important or unimportant

working class: people who do paid manual or industrial work

Index

activism 4-5, 15-19, 21, 25, 27-28, 31, 34-35, 42-43

campaigning 15, 17, 35, 43

Caribbean 6-7, 22-25, 30, 34-35, 37-41

civil rights 4, 15, 17, 19, 34, 42

Commonwealth 22

communism 16, 19, 21

feminism 15, 31, 43-46

inequality 27, 35

journalism 14-16, 30-34

King Jr, Dr Martin Luther 4, 18, 42

multiculturalism 37

New York 8-9, 20

Parks, Rosa 4, 18

protests 15, 17-18, 42

racism 5, 21, 27, 31, 37, 45-46

West Indian Gazette 28, 30-34, 38, 40, 45

Windrush Generation 23-24